Sybie,
Wishing you...
celebrations from the soul!!.

love,
Dede
10/17/2006

Celebrations
from the Soul
An Inspirational Sourcebook for Personal Entertaining

Dedra D. Faine

Celebrations *from the* Soul

An Inspirational Sourcebook for Personal Entertaining

DEDICATION

I dedicate this book to my husband, partner and best
friend Roger – thank you for your love, patience, support
and belief in my dreams. I thank God for giving me such a
wonderful husband whose spirit of patience and kindness
has been a blessing to me. I look forward to continuing to
walk through this wonderful journey of life with you.
I love you.

To my precious angels – Govan and Lauren. You are
both truly a blessing in my life and my biggest inspiration.
I thank God for giving me two beautiful children with
wonderful kind spirits that bring me constant joy. Mommy
adores and loves you so so much!

For information about special discounts for bulk purchases, please contact **GoLo Communications Book Sales: (504) 481-6779**

GoLo Communications
609 Metairie Road, #227
Metairie, LA 70005

Library of Congress Control Number: 2006927866

ISBN 0-9786382-0-4

10 9 8 7 6 5 4 3 2 1

Cover and interior Design: Alexandra Wesley

Editor: Diana Spindler-Jones

Every effort has been made to contact the photographers whose work is reproduced in this volume.

Photographs:

Bob Dalton, pages 1•2•3•4•10•12•24•26•27•30•32
    33•37•37•38•40•42•43 & Cover
Rodney Bailey (Courtesy of Windows Catering Company)
    pages 6•7•27•31•37•41•50•51•66
Corlessia Daniel, page 61

Printed in China

CONTENTS

WELCOME TO
MIDDLEBURG
Est. 1787

As a young girl, I spent many summers with my grandparents and extended family in the small quaint town of Middleburg, Virginia. Middleburg is a jewel of a town with rolling hills of beautiful countryside that for years has welcomed many people that come for antiquing, horse racing and to enjoy the historic inns.

During those summer days I spent most of my time with my grandmother Marlow, a beautiful, feisty, nurturing, and spiritual woman who loved her family. She worked for a family at a local farm in Upperville, Virginia. Her days were spent cooking and taking care of their home. During those times I watched my grandmother prepare and create dining pleasures and decorations for family celebrations. Grandma made those days so special. She took pride in her work as she helped the family entertain. She brought the same elaborate details into her own home when she entertained. Her talents will always be a legacy in our family. During celebrations like Thanksgiving I engage the spirits of past generations, namely my grandmother Marlow, in my entertaining.

Grandma Marlow's entertaining was a family trait and was practiced in my parent's home. My mom would enlist us for spring-cleaning anytime during the year in preparation. From getting curtains cleaned, polishing the silver and brass, and ordering flowers to putting together the menu with my father, who is the official "chef" of our family, so the list went. All of this preparation was done so our home could welcome our very special guests.

In my early twenties I discovered that the sense for entertaining I inherited is a deep-rooted part of my soul. Through my life journey I know that a stronger spiritual perspective of self-understanding in a deeper consciousness will enable oneself to produce Celebrations from the Soul.

"One of the greatest gifts that you can give to yourself and to others around you is to appreciate who you are.

Embrace the good in your past.

Illuminate the true essence of your spirit today.

Shine your unique light into the world. "

- Dedra Faine

Celebrations from the Soul gives you the ability to celebrate your past, be in the present and look forward to your future. When celebrating in this manner, you are able to discover what speaks to your spirit by tapping into your own sense of personal style. In addition, it enables you to be reflective of your family traditions and regional customs and welcome them into your celebrations. Incorporating these treasures into your entertainment environment will feed your soul. This is a wonderful way to honor your guests by revealing your spirit and making a true connection with them.

After many years of planning parties, I found that I better serve my clients by helping them create an atmosphere that is reflective of their inner spirit. We are all unique in our own wonderful ways. My goal is to assist you in creating and designing entertainment experiences that will capture the essence of who you are and share your wonderful story. I truly believe that if you project what is meaningful to your soul in everything you do, then it will come back to you in return.

Today, resources are widely available in different forums to show us examples of lavish and stunning parties. You often see many examples of star-studded events in written publications and on your television. It is wonderful to have such great resources at your fingertips; however, don't forget that your guests want to feel a part of your unique world. It is essential that we do not lose ourselves in other people's stories — your story is unique. Tap into your individual spirit and put your own spin on the party to truly welcome and embrace your guests.

I have created a three-step process to help you capture and create your own Celebration from the Soul. The first step is to understand your own personal entertainment design needs and what really speaks to your soul. There is a questionnaire that you will fill out that describes four different entertaining design scenarios: (1) Grande Dame – Elegant, (2) Voyager – Worldly, (3) Modish – Urban Glamour and (4) Town and Country – Casual Elegance. This questionnaire can be used as a tool to help you pick out things that stimulate your visual senses as well as your personal style and background.

The second and third steps are to help you add special touches that reflect elements of your uniqueness by answering questions in reference to your family traditions and regional culture and celebrations.

While we often know what makes us feel good in bits and pieces, this is your opportunity to create your distinctive myriad of details and capture the big picture of you. This will open doors and allow you to share your uniqueness along to others during your entertainment experiences. By walking through this process you will understand the beauty of Celebrating from the Soul.

Grande
Dame

VOYAGER

MODISH

TOWN &
COUNTRY

INVITING
Soulful Elements
INTO YOUR EVENT

WHAT IS THE CELEBRATION?

*W*e are going to plan a party that can be used in any theme, with any budget, place and guests — it is called your "Soul Celebration." In this celebration you are going to pull out all the elements that speak to your spirit and showcase them. As you go through these steps, you can use this process for all your parties. Whether you are hosting a fabulous event for yourself or for someone else, you can use this book as a guide to capture the "guest of honor." At the end of the day, when your spirit is pampered, your soul is pleased. I cannot think of a better way to have a party. So let's get started!

Design

*H*ave you ever walked into a fabulous party or a well decorated room and it spoke to your spirit? I have been to many places where the atmosphere is pampering to my spirit and I always try to capture that moment visually in my mind. So when I entertain I am able to incorporate things that I have seen and still add my own twists or personal touches. My goal as a lifestyle coach is to always embrace the desires of your heart that pamper your spirit. I have created four different "design characteristics" for entertaining atmospheres that can help you to capture a look that pleases your spirit. These four categories are not meant to pigeonhole you into one category or a particular design style. It is truly a way to visualize the perspectives on different entertainment design styles.

Quiz:
YOUR ENTERTAINMENT DESIGN STYLE

*F*irst, as you take this quiz, you must let go of all your boundaries and step into a world where everything is feasible — you just have to make choices on what you want to do. You will answer each question and envision yourself with the ability and resources to do whatever your heart desires. Take a moment and fill out the questionnaire. Once you have finished the questionnaire you will tally the results on the "tally form" and they will direct you to your design style, contained in the pages following the questionnaire. This is a fun and enlightening process, so enjoy it as you discover the entertainment design style that delights your spirit.

Determine Your Individual Entertaining Style

1. **If you had a special anniversary celebration, the ideal off-site location to host the party would be:**
    a.   A five star hotel
    b.   An outdoor party out on the ocean
    c.   A trendy club
    d.   A chateau in the country

2. **Your significant other invites you for a vacation getaway. What city would you prefer?**
    a.   Venice, Italy
    b.   Lake Tahoe, Nevada
    c.   South Beach, Miami
    d.   London, England

3. **You are entertaining special clients at your home. You display which flower arrangements?**
    a.   White roses presented extravagantly
    b.   Bamboo plants surrounded by exotic orchids
    c.   White tulips in clear rectangle vases
    d.   A floral arrangement from your own personal garden

4. **You are celebrating Thanksgiving or a similar holiday with family and friends. In what type of setting would you like to entertain?**
    a.   A sit-down dinner for 25 with a chef and waiter to assist you and your guests with every need
    b.   A barbecue on the beach and you would tell your friends to come and be casual
    c.   An intimate setting with no more than six people with non-traditional dishes
    d.   At a quaint inn or restaurant that features a specialty menu for the occasion

5. **You have the honor of picking a band or performer for your big birthday bash. You would hire:**
    a.   A big band or orchestra capable of playing a variety of music
    b.   Theme music (e.g. Caribbean – Steel Drums)
    c.   Hot Celebrity DJ
    d.   Jazz Performer

6. **You win a shopping spree to decorate your bedroom. Where would you go to shop?**
   a. Hire a designer — you want a skilled person to do your decorating
   b. Go to boutiques that feature culturally diverse worldly treasures
   c. Go to a stores that features contemporary furniture
   d. Antique shopping

7. **You are throwing a huge party to celebrate a prestigious award given to your significant other. You would…?**
   a. Go to a new local five star restaurant featuring a premier chef that will prepare a gourmet meal for this occasion
   b. Invite co-workers, family members and friends over to your home and celebrate with good wine and hors d'œuvres
   c. Get the VIP section at a hot club and throw a celebration with friends and family
   d. Go to your local country club and have everything done on-site to your exact specifications with two other couples

8. **You have just landed a huge contract where you have the option to live in the following places. Which would you choose?**
   a. Paris, France
   b. Sydney, Australia
   c. San Francisco, California
   d. Greenwich, Connecticut

9. **You have a choice to pick out a special piece of art for your home. You would choose:**
   a. A one-of-a-kind sculptured piece of crystal
   b. Unique African Sculpture
   c. Andy Warhol Painting
   d. 18th Century Painting

10. **You have just finished a major project and you have the weekend off. What would you do?**
    a. Have a dip and clip day (royal spa treatment)
    b. Spend a quiet restful weekend venturing out to have a picnic at a lake
    c. Fly to New York to let your hair down and party, party, party!
    d. Have a sleepy weekend at café's and browsing through antique shops

11. **Your best friend comes into town and you want to take her out and your time is limited.**
You would take her:
   a.   To a famous restaurant in your city
   b.   On a tour of the city
   c.   To a club for dancing
   d.   To a sporting event

12. **You are invited to a fund-raiser. You would bid on what silent auction item?**
   a.   Pair of Louis XV French chairs
   b.   An Italian motor scooter
   c.   An autographed jersey of a mega super star athlete
   d.   Local artist picture

13. **You are invited to a spa with a friend. What type of spa day would you pick?**
   a.   Go to the finest resort in the country to do spa treatments and lectures on preserving your body
   b.   Wellness spas (yoga, hike)
   c.   Silent Retreat to connect to your inner spirit
   d.   Go to a spa that features the most innovative body wrap and massage treatments

14. **You have hired a real estate agent to help you find your dream home.**
What would you describe as your dream home?
   a.   Refurbished home built in the late 1800s
   b.   A three-level beach front home
   c.   Penthouse floor in a top metropolitan city
   d.   A country estate

15. **You are on the hunt for a fabulous china pattern.**
What would you choose?
   a.   A monogrammed 18 kt. gold embossed traditional pattern
   b.   An earth tone bohemian themed pattern
   c.   A sleek white pattern with black outer lines
   d.   A beautiful floral antique set

16. **You have an invitation made for your special celebration. It looks like:**
    a. Hand scripted invitation on the finest cotton paper
    b. An invitation created for a theme – a party on the beach would have an invitation filled with sand and sea shells
    c. Keep it light and invite all of your guests via phone
    d. Engraved invitation featuring your personal monogram

17. **If you had to choose a theme for your birthday party, which would you choose?**
    a. A vintage cocktail party
    b. A candlelit evening soirée on the beach
    c. A black and white themed party with a splash of hot pink
    d. A wine tasting party

18. **If you had to have one particular cocktail featured at your soirée – What would it be:**
    a. The finest champagne
    b. Martini bar featuring a specialty potion themed towards your party
    c. Imported beer
    d. Wine tasting (flights)
    e. Non-alcoholic specialty punch

19. **If you were planning a wedding for yourself or a special person in your life and needed linen for ten tables:**
    a. You have the table linen custom made especially for the event with the family monogram
    b. You pull together a hodgepodge of linens you already have that are unique and have special meaning to the bride and groom?
    c. You go to your local rental company and rent their specialty linen that has a non-traditional presentation
    d. You go to a linen specialty shop and purchase ten white cotton linens so they can be used in the future

20. **If you had to host a special event at your home that features some type of educational reference which would you choose?**
    a. Wine connoisseur giving a wine tasting and brief lecture on international wines
    b. An event that features "The Art of Being Stress Free" with a spiritual teacher and masseuse
    c. Local chef teaching guests on how to prepare special low-fat delectables
    d. A cigar party that features different cigars around the world with live rollers to teach you how to roll your own cigar presented with brandy

WHAT DOES THIS MEAN?

Step 1: Tally up your score

You can use the following chart as you tally up all of the A's, B's, C's and D's. Please note that if you answered E to any question – it can be used within any category; therefore, it does not count. Please total the numbers that you have in each section.

	1	2	3	4	5	6	7	8	9	10	11	12	13	14	15	16	17	18	19	20	TOTAL
A																					
B																					
C																					
D																					

Step 2: Understanding your score

You may have the majority of your answers in one particular category that suits you or you may be scattered in different areas. In that case, pull in the different elements that speak to you throughout the categories. Something should materialize that speaks to you and sparks ideas on the type of entertainment design that you would incorporate into your party. Remember these categories are not meant to put you in a box — they are meant to give you a description of details that could be incorporated throughout your entertainment experience, and you can pick and choose whatever specifically fits your needs. The next few pages will give you visual and descriptive examples of what that category design looks like within an entertainment environment.

If the majority of your answers are **A** your style is **Grande Dame**. Literally Grande Dame is described as a woman who has reached a high level of status in her adult life, whether it is in her career, society, charitable works or other deeds. Women that are characterized as Grande Dame are regal in their stature and style and they encompass the finest of prestige. These terms are the perfect match for the most glamorous, diva-like party of them all.

You evoke an entertaining design style that represents your love of handpicked elements of superlative quality within the presentation of your celebration. If you are in the Grande Dame category you enjoy formal affairs, filled with the finest champagne and caviar, and classic gourmet presentations. Your stately accessories include luxurious china, candelabras, taper candles, taffeta, silk, linen, over the top flowers displayed in magnificent fashion, sterling silver, gold trays and table ware. You like to have your affairs in locations that are unique in character due to their flawless service, grandness and opulent décor. You like to have parties where the required dress is formal attire such as white-tie. You love classical music presentations whether it is the symphony or a big band. You want your guests to walk into the lap of luxury when they enter your affair.

If the majority of your answers are **B** your style is **Voyager**. As a traveler who likes to adventure, sightsee and enjoy the magnificence of the earth and its surroundings, you represent the multi-dimensional individual that is connected to all areas of the earth. You like to showcase the beauty of the earth in your entertainment design presentations. Your unique celebration would pull in discoveries from your travels coupled with different textures, fabrics and accessories that blend the right elements of discovery and pleasures of life.

You like your entertaining environments to be casual in presentation with a peaceful aura. Your ideal locations would include a view of the mountains or beach, the sounds of a roaring fireplace and the look and sound of white capped ocean waves as they rush toward the shore. Your food presentations would be presented in fascinating presentation that represents your regional thematic party. You love the beauty of a sunset. You would include a band that features the beat of the worldly place that you are showcasing. Your accessories could include candles, crystals, stones, sculptures, exotic flowers, bamboo plants and teak wood and any other earthly treasures. You would showcase Indian, African, Moroccan and other fabrics from around the world. In addition soft linens and organza in earthy tones would be a great accent for your affair. You want your guests to be embraced by the peace and beauty of the earth and all the embellishments that come with it.

If the majority of your answers are **C** your style is *Modish*. Modish is characterized as trendy, current and always in the know of what is the latest and greatest in entertaining from places to go, foods to serve and the right décor – including colors, types of serving pieces and the list goes on.

You are a hip party planner that wants to always set trends. Whether it is in your décor style, the new drinks to serve or the most current music – you are constantly one step ahead of the others. To compliment your urban lifestyle you like very clean and simple yet fashionable entertainment presentations. An ideal site for you to host a party would be at a trendy club, in your sleek styled high rise apartment or new chic art gallery. You like to be in settings that are fast paced near trendy restaurants, hot clubs and bustling cafes. You like geometrical shapes and lots of bold color to compliment your oftentimes stark white background. At your party – you like to bring in your favorite DJ of choice to play current songs along with pulling out some old classics and giving them a whole new spin and life. When people come to your affair you want them to be inspired and re-energized by lively conversations, sleek décor, sophisticated food presentations, wonderful music and spirited dancing. They will leave your parties wanting more and looking forward to the next hot party.

If the majority of your answers are **D** your style is *Town & Country*. This style embodies classic and traditional styling that is often reflective of towns where you will find an array of antique shops, close-knit traditions, historical artifacts and famous inns. It is often described as a place where you can take refuge and leave the traffic and stress of the world behind.

You like to pull out all of your finest pieces when you entertain. You love to display your great grandmothers serving platter, or your great aunts fine silver. Tradition runs very deep for you; therefore, you pull out all of your families finest when entertaining. You have a casual elegance in presentation. Although your display may look formal you want people to relax and enjoy the comforts of your entertaining environment. Your ideal party would be located at your home or sometimes you may want to invite your guests out to a lovely luncheon or tea at a famous local inn where you know the chef personally. You love to dine on antique china patterns, silver and beautiful lace and linen. Pulling out your families silver cups for a party at your home featuring "mint juleps" is your cup of tea. You love to visit wineries and collect them from your local region to share with your many guests that come to your home. You love to celebrate during the holidays and collect many special pieces throughout the years to create beautiful inviting displays. You want guests to feel a part of your home and to leave with the spirit of your family and its traditions.

Grande Dame

CHAMPAGNE SOIRÉE

A Grande Dame party can be thrown for 500 people or as few as two people. In this case we had an intimate party for four. It was Grande Dame at its best. The theme décor was gold and ivory. We added a punch of "Diva" with the leopard chairs that were used for seating. The attire for the evening was white-tie and evening gowns. The glass table with its gold legs were adorned with two beautiful ornate gold runners that crisscrossed at the center. The table setting was created with a gold charger and a china pattern that was ivory with gold-gilded edges. The forks used were sterling silver with a gold base.

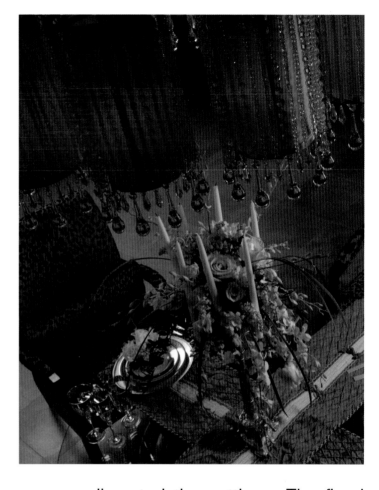

In addition to the flatware, gold etched crystal glasses complimented the setting. The floral arrangement was presented in a dramatic fashion displayed with an array of lilies and roses in a gold candelabra. Let me tell you, if you ask your guests to come in formal attire for an intimate dinner party it is truly something special. On special occasions, bring in the waitstaff, the caterers, and, of course, all of the bells and whistles — it is a great feeling to treat yourself and your guests in such an exquisite manner. After this party you and your guests will be walking on your tip toes for days.

VOYAGER

large floor pillows fabrics

teak exotic florals

eclectic

Outdoors incense teak

animal prints relaxed wood

Beach sculptures mountain

Roaring Fireplace worldly

sounds of the ocean earth tones

worldly Teak exotic floral

organza comfortable

wood Sunset crystals cozy

Indian/African/Moroccan incense

soft linens organza candles

Roaring Fireplace

sounds of the ocean

crystals earth tones

beach sculptures

BOOK CLUB WITH FRIENDS

A soft warm inviting environment was set in front of a stone fireplace with a beautiful fire that created a glow within the room. A beautiful ornate rug was displayed in front of the fireplace to create a warm textured backdrop for the seating area. Burgundy silk rectangular pillows were used for the book club members seating. A centerpiece with wood sticks, fresh red roses, and dried red rose balls were displayed around three glass lanterns with sage-colored candles. The softness of the candles illuminating against the warmth of the fireplace was the perfect voyager setting that was a welcoming, relaxed environment. I cannot think of a better way to be with friends, discussing your book of choice, life events and, of course, telling secrets that do not leave the circle, all while drinking red wine and eating special hors d'œuvres made just for the occasion.

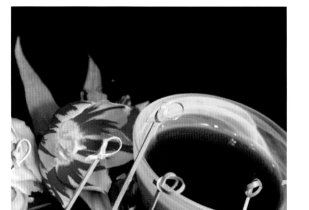

Marcie's Birthday Party
A TROPICAL CELEBRATION

*A*tropical soiree was created to celebrate Marcie's birthday. Given Marcie's Jamaican heritage, we created a party that was festive and showcased a tropical theme. The room was filled with bright jovial colors like mango, lime, and fuchsia. We brought in large bamboo and tropical plants to accent the room. When you walk into the room it instantly gives you an island feel that makes you want to start doing the rumba. We kept the décor simple with bright candles displayed in different sizes and colors, large green leaves and orchids as an accent. The drink of choice was a peach colada (we also served virgin coladas). We wanted a rich display of food that was hearty yet simple in an exotic presentation. The party was all that we planned it to be — an evening of upbeat festivities, socializing, dancing, good food and lots of love.

MODISH

high style faST paCE

bold coloring fine lines

stark white small spaces modern art

trendy

white clean linessmall spaces

urban glamour stark whitemodern art

fine linesbold

high style trendy

mall spaces

hot clubshigh style

Fashionable Restaurants

fine lines urban glamo

fast pace high rise café Hot Clubs

high style café bold coloring art

hot clubsstyleclean lines

stark white modern art

urban glamour faST paCE

After Work Martini Night
FEATURING THE BLUE WONDER

You call all your friends to come over after work for what you theme as the "Blue Wonder" happy hour. You tell them to put on their club attire because afterwards, you all are heading out to dance the night away. Everyone comes over in their festive attire and you have set a room that is part "club," part "jazzy," part "nouveau" all in your small space. Your friends will be really impressed. You have turned your black-and-chrome furniture themed apartment into a blue oasis.

You play the right music, you hire a hip bartender, and you bring in all of the right accessories. You hang blue beads behind your bar, you have the coolest candles that are thirty-six inches tall scattered in black and blue, you bring in beautiful white tulips in a modular vase in order to embrace the season.

You provide food that is chic, hip, and fun. This is not a whole lot of fussiness, just the right elements placed perfectly to create the look that you want. Guess what — after you pull this together, I bet all of your friends will be asking, "Is happy hour at your house this week?" And nine times out of ten, you will never make it to the club because your place will be happening. Have fun, and work it out!!!

Town & Country

EVENING PARTY

As the fall enters into the horse country area of Virginia, it is always the perfect time to have an outdoor party. The skies are clear and there is a little nip in the air, yet the crispness of the evening makes you enjoy being out in the greatness of the season. Fall is my favorite time of the year and it is the perfect time to have an outdoor tented affair to enjoy the wonders of the richly colored foliage. Creating a warm environment within your home with a fireplace and serving hot totties for the adults and warm apple cider with cinnamon sticks for children is always a nice retreat to come into from the outdoors on a special night such as this.

TEA ON THE TERRACE

To give a little girl a special tea party is always a special treat. When my daughter turned five we had a "mother-daughter-princess" tea party and all of the girls had to wear their special party dresses. It was such a wonderful occasion that all the mothers talked about for a long time after. We recreated a special tea setting for Lauren and once again it was so much fun bringing all of the frilly and dainty details into the party that were still very tasteful.

The setting that we created was on a terrace where we used an antique iron table and two chairs and a complimentary server. On the table we displayed an antique miniature tea set that was appropriate for Lauren. We had an antique cup and saucer along with all of the fixings. The tablecloth used was a silk underlay and covered with tulle. Lauren's chairs were covered in white tulle, which was tied in the back with a large silk ribbon. Then we accented the bow with lush pink roses. Now for the goodies, we served special butterfly and flower cookies that pulled in all of the theme colors of pink, lilac, and yellow. The most special treats displayed were the jumbo petit fours that were covered in a yellow fondant icing and decorated with pink flowers. The petit fours were displayed on a two-tier silver dessert tray and filled with the most precious pink flowers. When your little someone walks into a room and her face brightens up you know that you have created the most perfect setting. I know with my little girl, the room set-up was nice, but the special treats that came along with it went a long way. As a nice giveaway, little nosegays (small bouquets of fresh flowers) that compliment the rest of the floral displays at the party are always a special touch. Little girls and big girls love that special touch.

Now that you a have an image of what each category looks like you can see what speaks to you visually. Review the categories that fall into that particular design scheme and that will give you the elements that help to bring that particular design style to life. Then you can bring in the little details that can illuminate your own personal design style. For example, if you have the majority of your answers in the traditional category and the next category that you like is the worldly/ethnic category, you can still bridge those two design categories. I have a client who is very traditional in her decorating style; however, she loves to travel and bring beautiful pieces from around the world into her home. She was hosting a Thanksgiving dinner for twelve people. In order to help her truly unveil who she was to her guests, we incorporated the worldly treasures into her entertaining. We fashioned a table that featured a striking textured cloth that she found during her travels in India. The cloth had rich tones of plum, sky blue, black, and beige in a rich texture ornate pattern. We used it as a runner on the table and filled it with gourds, miniature pumpkins, and dried corncobs to offset the arrangements featuring dried flowers, leaves, and oranges. Ornate candle holders decorated with Egyptian figures in rich tones were filled with plum candle sticks that illuminated the table. We still used her very traditional china pattern and linens that had dried flowers as the napkin holders. The table was a masterpiece in that it had a traditional look that showcased the host by featuring her worldly/ethnic treasures, and the guests were able to capture the true sense of the hostess' essence.

Have fun with your design style in pulling out all of the elements that feature who you are. You will discover that you are a full spectrum of many things. The ability to bring it all to fruition during your entertaining experience will be a delight to your soul.

INVITING IN *Family Traditions*

Now that you have an image of your own personal entertaining style, we are going to venture into your family traditions and dig deeper into the details of what your entertaining experience will accentuate. Rituals ingrained from celebrations have evolved from the beginning of time. As you create your own entertaining environment reflective of your spirit, family traditions are a great resource to pull from. We are often privy to the treasures of family traditions as young children. As we move into adulthood we can embrace family traditions in our entertainment environment, and embellish them with our own special touches to make them unique.

I was blessed to have many family traditions passed down to me from my parents and grandparents over the years. As an adult, I incorporate the great treasures that started with my grandparents into my entertaining — especially during family celebrations like Thanksgiving, Christmas, and Easter. What keeps me grounded and connected to my family is my guests not only are getting a sense of me and my immediate family, but also of past generations and the legacies that they have passed on. My grandmothers and my parents were very influential with who I am today and that is evident in my entertaining. My dad was the decorator in our home. During Christmas time he would decorate the outdoors, the trees

and all of the other special details around the home. Each year we would wait with excitement to see what the theme of the year was going to be. Then he would always recruit me as his little helper, which was a great bonding time for us. My mother's extra care around the home and putting the final touches on the home taught me a lot about entertaining and preparation as well as keeping a great time line. My parents helped shape who I am today as a lifestyle professional and I am grateful to them for that.

My grandmother Daniel was the greatest cook ever and her special recipes were always "front and center" at any holiday gathering at my home. Grandma made the best sweet potatoes with marshmallows that I have ever tasted. She seasoned everything just so and the love that was put into each step of her cooking made her food taste even better. Many of her recipes — cornbread stuffing, sweet potatoes, cherry cobbler — are staples at my table today. And her special recipes and dishes are being passed on to our next generation. My grandmother Marlow's family gatherings were formal. She took extra time in making sure that each detail was planned with ultimate care. During holidays, she always pulled out her finest linens and polished silver along with a host of other fine serving pieces. My grandfather, who we always referred to as "King Tut," was a gentlemen's gentlemen and was dapper in his red velvet vest alongside my other relatives who came in their holiday finest. The atmosphere was filled with the smells of my grandmother's famous country Virginia cured ham and delicious homemade eggnog. The sound of Nat King Cole singing soulful Christmas classics filled the air as we all delighted in the joyful spirit-filled occasion. The adults sat in the dining room where my grandmother had made a lovely presentation. The children sat in the kitchen, which she would make extra special for us with pretty linens. I'll never forget the displays of coconut candies and pecans, nectarines, and fruit cake used in her displays. My holiday entertaining experiences are filled with the same elements. I find it comforting to include these treasured activities from my life in my holiday parties. My children will receive the good in my past through such celebrations.

What I need you to do now is to think about your celebrations as a child. Use all of your senses to reveal what stood out for you as a child. Go back to family gatherings, think about the food, decorations, special traditions that warm your soul. Whatever they may be, take some time and jot them down so you can pull it into your entertaining today. I always feel that home is where the heart is. You could be hundreds of miles away from any family member; however, if you incorporate special traditions from your family, it takes you home, brings a sense of comfort, and embraces the times of unconditional love.

For some of you, entertaining may not have been a major factor in your childhood. However, if you are reading this book it means that it does have a special place in your heart, and that you want to create something with your unique stamp on it. This is your opportunity to create your own legacies. For example, during the holidays you could invite your friends and neighbors over for a cookie exchange and bring the special treats to local shelters and sing carols to the residents. That is something that you can carry on to the next generation. Use your imagination and bring whatever speaks to your heart and soul to the surface. Relish in the joy that it will bring to you and others around you.

Remember, legacies from the past are true gifts that help shape future generations. Embrace them in your celebrations today, honor your past and present and build the bridge to the future. Take this time to reflect on your family traditions. I have established a questionnaire to help you to think about your family traditions and what means the

most to you so you can integrate it in your entertaining experience. Going through the following steps will help you tap into your thoughts on the topic of family traditions.

It's now time to go somewhere quiet and reflect on your past family celebrations. Allow at least ten minutes for you to meditate. Close your eyes for the first couple of minutes. Eliminate present thoughts, outside sound, and just be silent. After sitting for a while, allow yourself to listen to your inner voice. Think about your family traditions and embrace all that is good in them. Think about your childhood — favorite

dishes, holidays, places, celebrations, toys. If something puts a smile on your face, embrace it. If it brings bad memories, let it go. Remember, we are embracing the good in our pasts.

Now that you have gotten centered and are reflecting on your family and its entertaining traditions, let's see how we can capture the good in your family traditions and bring them into your celebratory experiences today.

Family Traditions Questionnaire

1. As a child were there any special holiday experiences that stand out for you today? Why?

   _____

   _____

   _____

2. Who was instrumental in your life in giving you a sense of unconditional love and comfort? How can you honor that person during your entertaining experiences?

   _____

   _____

   _____

3. Was there any particular food that brought you comfort today?

   _____

   _____

   _____

4. What do family gatherings mean to you?

   _____

   _____

   _____

5. If you could look forward to future generations as they celebrate, what family ritual would you like to see passed down from you?

_____

_____

_____

6. If you could change a family tradition to put your own spin on it, what would it be?

_____

_____

_____

7. What type of music did you listen to as a child that would give your guests a direct connection to your past?

_____

_____

_____

8. Were your family celebrations formal, semi-formal or casual? Describe the decor.

_____

_____

_____

Okay, you have connected with your past family celebrations and rituals — what do you do from here? Good question. Now you are going to pull all of the elements that you just wrote about into your soul celebration. For example, in question two, I asked you who gave you unconditional love in your past and how you can honor them in your celebrations.

An example for me would be my great aunt Anna and her husband, my great uncle Hansen. They were very rich in character. They lived in the heart of the city of Baltimore, Maryland in a beautiful brownstone. Although they lived in the city, their home had a town and country flair. The home was decorated with antiques, beautiful paintings and filled with lots of small delicate items that as a kid I knew that it was to look at and not to touch. The four-story building was large and had a lot of secret doors and compartments. When I was young, those doors were a big mystery to me and my brothers used to tease me to make them seem spooky. I now realize the compartments were just storage closets. The imagination of a child can make things seem so big.

Also, Aunt Anna and Uncle Hansen had a small grocery store in their neighborhood. They allowed me and my brothers and sisters to go there and help ourselves to the many goodies in the store. As a child, going to their home full of such distinctive character and their graciousness made us feel very special.

Now when I reflect on the many times that we spent there during the holidays, I see that we celebrated at our family's highest level. I realize they celebrated in ways that were reflective of the '30s era of Hollywood glamour. So when I celebrate and I am feeling like I want to put on a fabulous party, I bring my Aunt Anna's and Uncle Hansen's beautiful spirits into my party by celebrating those two people who were instrumental in exposing me to not only the finer things in life, but the ability to celebrate life in the grandest fashion.

INCORPORATING
Regional Culture

Just as we use our family traditions in our celebrations, we also can use our regional culture in our entertaining. Wherever you are, you can include the culture of the region as an integral part of your entertaining experience.

I lived in the wonderful city of New Orleans for three years. I gained so much knowledge from living in that soulful city of abundant culture, style, gracious hospitality, and rich and fervent history. It is truly one of the entertaining capitals of America. As a native Virginian and a new resident of that city, New Orleanians impressed me with their hospitality from day one. People shared with me the richness of their city — they opened their doors to my family and welcomed us wholeheartedly by sharing their spirits. It truly was a gift that I will cherish forever.

Nine times out of ten, New Orleanians' acts of kindness are evident in their inviting people to celebrations — family, friends, clients, co-workers, school associates, and new members of their community. Whether it is at their home or some other locale, they show caring through some form of entertaining. A typical week in New Orleans could look like this: Sunday — invite guests to church, then to Sunday brunch; Monday — invite over for dinner featuring red beans and rice, a New Orleans staple; Tuesday — special ladies luncheon; Wednesday — kids' birthday party after school at City Park (by the way, they invite not only the class, but the whole grade); Thursday — dinner out at a great restaurant; Friday — local sporting event, then a fish dinner with family (this is a very traditional Catholic city); Saturday — get your pick of birthday parties, fund-raiser galas, bar mitzvahs, anniversaries, crawfish boils, and the list goes on. This is their way of humbly revealing layers of themselves to their guests through their own sense of personal servitude, entertainment, and hospitality. They have mastered the art of capturing the bounty and culture of their city and their own sense of personal style coupled with their family traditions into each of their entertaining experiences.

As a transplant from Virginia living in New Orleans, I often return to my native roots of Washington, D.C. and its surrounding areas of Virginia and Maryland as a source of inspiration for my entertaining. Growing up there, we often looked forward to the blooming 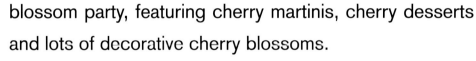 of the cherry blossoms every spring. It was the coming out party for a new season as the beautiful flowers throughout the area came to life. This time was often marked as a rite of passage for the people who lived in the area because it was a time to come out of the hibernation of winter and to enjoy the beautiful weather and surroundings that embodied the city. In such a wonderful region as the New Orleans area, ripe with celebrations of cultural traditions and history, I love to give my new friends a sense of who I am and the regional perspective from which I come by incorporating my regional culture into my celebrations. For example, as many people are enjoying crawfish boils around New Orleans during early spring, I have a cherry blossom party, featuring cherry martinis, cherry desserts and lots of decorative cherry blossoms.

I'm not sure where my next destination will be as I move forward in time; however, I do know that I will bring wonderful celebrations from New Orleans with me. So for all you emigrants, take heed of each location that you live in and bring it forth with you. Not only will it enrich your life but the lives of those around you. For those of you who do not move around a lot, embrace your city and culture — find the heartbeat of your city and bring that into your celebrations. Whether it is a small town or large city, your hometown is unique, so celebrate it! Where you were born and how you were raised plays an important part in what makes up your spirit. By celebrating your birthplace and other places that you have journeyed you are celebrating your life.

Regional Culture Questionnaire

1.   Where are you from? What about that region brings you peace?

_____

_____

_____

2.   Are there any regional festivals or celebrations that you can incorporate into your party?

_____

_____

_____

3.   What is unique about the weather in your town/city?

_____

_____

_____

4.   Are there any historical attributes in your town/city?

_____

_____

_____

5.   If someone came from out of town – what would be the one place that you would have to show them in your town/city? Why?

_____

_____

_____

6.   What makes your town/city unique from any other place in the world?
     How can you celebrate that uniqueness?

_____

_____

_____

7.   If you had to move today, what aspect of your hometown would you want to bring with you because it has made you a better person?

_____

_____

_____

A Celebration FROM THE Soul

You have answered questions and have gone through the process of pulling out the design, family traditions, and regional cultures – tools that can embody your soul celebration. While walking through this process, you have visualized design elements that speak to you, you have pulled out the good from your family traditions and celebrations, and you have tapped into where you are from and what makes it unique in your eyes. It is finally time to have your *Soul Celebration* and shine your inimitable light into the world.

DDFaine–TIPS FOR PLANNING YOUR CELEBRATION

After many years of planning parties, when I finish pulling everything together, I always do a walkthrough of the room before the event begins and a wonderful feeling comes over me because I know the details that it took to pull it all together. I say my own personal "TA-DAAA!" to myself. In order to have these ta-da moments, I have to acknowledge that it takes a lot of good planning and special techniques to pull everything together. As you plan your celebration, you can use the following *"DDFaine Ta-Da"* tricks as your own personal resource.

I. Understand Your Honoree
DESIGN STYLE, FAVORITE THINGS, PASTIMES, MEMORIES, CULTURE

Nothing makes a person feel more special than when you have taken the extra time to understand who they are — their design style, favorite things, their likes and dislikes, favorite memories, their culture, hobbies, favorite foods and beverages — and incorporate it into their celebration.

II. Choose the Right Theme for Your Budget
THINGS TO CONSIDER TO KEEP WITHIN YOUR BUDGET

Pick a time of the day when food costs are less expensive. • Serve one specialty beverage instead of a full bar to keep costs lower. • If you are having a catered event, use their expertise in finding other vendors from florists to entertainment — they do these things on a daily basis and should have an ample amount of people they use and trust. Often times, when you are referred from another reputable company, they will work with you and your budget to accommodate your needs. • Always include a contingency amount for last minute items. Trust me, they do come up. • Lastly, if you can include waitstaff in your budget, it will make your evening much less hectic and you will be able to enjoy yourself. If you have to decide whether to have a great giveaway or waitstaff, go with the waitstaff. Your guests will enjoy your personal attention a lot more.

III. Design the Invitation
IMPORTANT THINGS TO REMEMBER FOR YOUR INVITATION

The invitation sets the tone for the party and often determines whether your guests will pick one party over the other. It is important to put some creative effort into thier design.

- ❏ Let guests know what attire is required.
- ❏ Proofread: celebration title, location, date, time, RSVP date, guests' names.
- ❏ If you are unsure of how to format your invitation, visit specialty stationary stores in person or online — there are tons of ideas out there that you can tap into.
- ❏ Remember to indicate if it is a surprise.
- ❏ Choose a unusual invitation size that does not look like your guests' other mail.
- ❏ At the post office, check the weight and make sure to apply enough postage.
- ❏ The post office also has a variety of stamps — pick one that compliments your event.
- ❏ Consider using a calligrapher — it truly will be a unique touch for your party.
- ❏ Have someone else proofread the invitation for you. Another trick is to read the invitation backward. You can catch typos that way.

Design Your Event

PLAN YOUR MENU

❑ Plan a stress-free menu that can be prepared ahead of time with little work the evening of your party. Remember, your guests want to enjoy your company. If you want a more elaborate meal, prepare some specialty dishes with your own flair and have the rest catered.

SELECT YOUR BEVERAGES FOR THE EVENING

❑ If you are serving non-alcoholic beverages, be creative in devising your concoction.

❑ You can always create a featured drink for the evening (e.g. your guest of honor loves the color blue, he loves the water and drinks gin — you create a drink called the "OceaOnic."

❑ If you are serving spirits like wine or champagne, go to your local wine and beverage store to enlist the help of the on-site experts in choosing the right wine pairings for your menu.

CREATE THE PERFECT AMBIANCE

❑ Candles, candles, candles — they always set the right mood and provide the most intimate lighting.

❑ Entertainment is crucial for setting the right mood for your party. Whether it is a great CD or a live jazz quartet — it is the one detail that sets the tone of the energy within your party. Take extra care in selecting your songs for the evening. You might want to start off slower and build up to a high energy level and then bring it back down for the end of the party. If you choose entertainment outside of music such as a magician or storyteller – remember to make sure that their performance times are at the right pulse points within your time line.

Establish a Time line

A good time line is crucial to any event and can be especially helpful when you are entertaining in your home. You want to write down the date, action, when it will be finished, and any special notes. I always like to send all of the vendors this same list so we can all be on the same page. Also, write a vendor list with names, contacts, delivery times and phone numbers. This will help keep everything organized on the day of your event.

Jewelry for the Event
LINENS, TABLEWARE, FLORALS, SERVING PIECES

I always call the accessories for the party your special jewels that you use as your accent.

❑ You may have plenty of tableware items to satisfy the numbers on your guest list, or if you don't, go to your local event rental company and have them deliver the accessories that you may need.

❑ Florals - you may be wonderful at creating your own flower arrangements, and that is great. If not, I suggest that you visit a florist at least two weeks ahead of time. and look over the inventory and pick out flowers that speak to all of your senses. Also, going to a florist that has plenty of flowers in his/her current inventory to choose from or a portfolio that matches your taste is very important.

❑ While you are in the process of designing and planning your party, keep your eyes open for visual accessories that speak to you — it could be jewelry from a street vendor that is a good accent for a napkin ring holder or a beautiful scarf that you may see that sets the tone for the colors of your party. Things around you can speak to you in various forms that can help stimulate your senses and help you as you create a sensational affair with its own special twists.

VI

VII Schedule a "Me" Day
ONE OF MY MOST IMPORTANT TA-DA TIPS

Get a manicure, pedicure, hairstyling and massage the day before your party. You want to look and feel your absolute best when you are entertaining.

Get Dressed 2 Hours Early VIII

When your first guest arrives you want to be there to greet him or her looking flawless, without a care in the world. You want to have a good time and enjoy your company. Problems may come up right before your party and you do not want to be caught off guard.

IX Have Fun

Remember, true hospitality is giving of your spirit when guests enter your home. Take care of yourself — feel beautiful and be relaxed. From the first guest's arrival to the last guest's departure, you want them to receive the blessings from the true essence of who you are. Enjoy!! There is no party like a party where you Celebrate from the Soul!

RECIPES

All recipes provided courtesy of Windows Catering Company with the exception of "The Blue Wonder".
DDFaine, LLC reminds you to drink responsibly.

PAELLA VALENCIA

Ingredients:
* 1/2 cup dry white wine
* 1 ts saffron (azafrán)
* Olive oil or cooking spray
* 1/2 cup chopped onion
* 1 cup long grain rice OR
* 1 cup yellow rice with saffron
* 1 red bell pepper
* 1 orange bell pepper
* 3 cups chicken stock
* 6 oz chicken breast, skinless
* 1/2 lb fresh shrimp
* 1 lb mussels
* 2 lb clams
* 2, 3 oz lobster tails
* 1/2 cup artichoke hearts
* 1 cup frozen peas
* 1/2 cup chopped tomato

> The smaller the clams, the better, since they cook faster and are easier to eat.

Pre-Cooking:
* Preheat oven to 350°
* Let peas defrost
* Chop the onion, tomato and bell peppers
* Peel shrimp
* Cut chicken into small cubes
* Scrub clams and mussels, discarding any that are already open

TO PEAL SHRIMP EASILY:

* Hold the shrimp so that you can grab it from the back and peel off the legs of the shrimp
* Peel off a piece of the shell around the head area
* Hold on to the head area of the shrimp and pull the tail, when done correctly the whole shell while come out

Directions:
* Coat the frying pan with cooking spray or olive oil
* Preheat the frying pan for one minute at med-high heat
* Sauté the onion 2-3 mins until limp and brown
* Add the rice, sauté until golden stirring so it won't burn
* Add the wine and saffron (if not already in the rice), stir until all the wine is absorbed
* Stir in the peppers
* Add 2 cups of chicken stock, 1/4 cup at a time stirring until the rice absorbs the stock (this will take a while)
* Add the last cup of chicken stock
* Add the cubed chicken
* Tuck the shrimp, clams, lobster and mussels into the rice
* Bake in the oven for 8-10 minutes until mussels open
* Add the peas, tomato and artichokes and bake for 2 more minutes
* Yields 4 Servings

GARLIC ROASTED PORK LOIN

Ingredients:
* 2 1/2 pounds pork roast
* 3 cloves garlic, sliced
* 2 1/2 cups white wine
* 3 tablespoons lemon juice
* 1/4 cup olive oil
* 3 onions, chopped
* 2 bay leaves
* 1 tablespoon dried thyme
* 1 teaspoon salt
* 1/2 teaspoon ground black pepper

Directions:
* Make slits in the roast and insert garlic slices
* Combine in a large plastic bag: wine, lemon juice, olive oil, onions, bay leaves, thyme, salt and pepper
* Add roast and marinate overnight in refrigerator
* Preheat oven to 350° F (175° C)
* Remove meat from marinade and roast until meat is no longer pink inside and thermometer reads 160° to 170° F (71° to 77° C)
* Yields 4 Servings

THE BLUE WONDER

Ingredients:
* 1 Part Vodka
* 2 Parts White Cranapple Juice
* 1 Part Blue Liqueur
* 1 tablespoon of lemon juice if you like a sour taste
* Twist of lemon

Directions:
* Combine all ingredients into a shaker
* Add ice
* Shake until frothy
* Pour into glasses and garnish with a twist of lemon
* Yields One Drink

LATTICE POTATO CHIP WITH CAVIAR AND CREME FRAICHE

Ingredients:
* 1 Idaho potato peeled and sliced 1/16" and set in water
* 2 cups peanut oil
* 4 oz. of creme fraiche or sour cream
* 1 or 2 oz. of caviar
* 2 to 3 chive laces minced
* 1 patch of wheat grass

> You may like to try beluga, ocetra, sevruga, american sturgeon or any other caviar or fish roe

Directions:
* Heat peanut oil to 350°
* Remove sliced potatoes from water and pat dry
* Place potatoes in hot oil and fry until golden brown
* Remove and place on paper towel, let cool for 1 min.
* Place small dollop of creme fraiche or sour cream on crisp potato slice and crown with small amount of caviar and minced chives
* Place on the wheat grass and serve to guests
* Yields 4 Serving

ACKNOWLEDGEMENTS

I do not stand alone in bringing this book to fruition. I want to extend my graditude to all of those that have helped me along the way:

Grandmothers Hannah B. Daniel and Kathleen G. Marlow: Their strength, integrity and great love for our family is a legacy that I will cherish forever. **James and Mary Daniel:** Thank you mom and dad for your constant belief, encouragement and always being my number one fans. You both have been wonderful to me and I am who I am today because of your love, dedication and unwavering support to help mold me, guide me as a Christian, mother, wife, daughter, sister and friend. Thank you both so much – I love you!!! **My siblings – Angela, Corlessia, JD, Forrest and Gregory:** You have all touched me and made me grow in so many ways. Angela thanks for teaching me to be the perfect host. Corlessia thanks for teaching me to stand up for what is right and be a strong business woman. JD thank you for your testimony years ago to tell me to put all of my Faith and Trust in God. From that day forward I have lived my life doing just that and it is the best word of advice that anyone has ever given me. I am eternally grateful. To Forrest my twin and soul mate – thank you for believing in me and for always being my knight and shining armor. To my special brother Gregory thank you for your love and treating me like a Queen. I love you all so much and I am able to do what I am doing today because of all of you. Thank you for your constant support and love. **My bestfriends – Kim, Lisa and Marcie:** It's great to go through your life and to find one best friend. I have been truly blessed with three unique best friends who I love dearly. Kim – thank you for your love, always being there when I need you and being my constant giggle partner. To know that I have you in my life – makes me sleep more comfortable at night (smile). Lisa – thank you for your love and constant support. You have always been my conscious, always a good listener, thank you for helping me to see the light and for helping me along to finish this book – I am forever grateful. Last but not least – Marcie – my sunshine and personal cheerleader - thank you for your love, friendship, your constant encouragement and being such a good energy source. You are truly special and I appreciate you. Thank you my sister friends – I love you all!!! **Frances Wallace (Aunt Pooh), Horace Marlow, Jr. (Uncle Junie) and Debra Jordan (Aunt Dee Dee):** Thank you all for your encouragement and helping me to pull together pictures for the book. **My mentor – Linda Higgison:** Your faith and trust in God that you bring forth in all that you do is my guideline as I walk on this journey to create my legacy as a business women in this world. **Erin LaMotte:** Thank you for always stepping up to the plate with a can do attitude. Your loyalty, dedication and great talents are just what the doctor ordered for DDFaine, LLC. You got the vision from day one and I am so happy to have you along for the ride. You are truly special and I look forward to creating great things with you on our team. **My New Orleans Friends – Andrea, Angele, Heather, Karen, Toni and the Metairie Park Country Day Family:** Thank you for your graciousness and true Southern Hospitality. Each and every one of you opened your arms, homes and hearts to our family and I am forever grateful. You are the inspiration of "Celebrations from the Soul" We love and miss you all!

The following person(s) or businesses have been instrumental in producing this book. I am very thankful and blessed to have each and everyone of them working on this project with me.

Alexandra Wesley
Freelance Graphic Design
amwesley@gmail.com

Phyllis Bridges
Yalik's Interior Design
1216 Cedrow Drive
High Point NC 27265

Raphael Eccolo
Designer/Consultant
14828 Baltimore Ave.
Laurel, Maryland 20707

Windows Catering Company
5724 General Washington Dr.
Alexandria, VA 22312

Kagan's Furniture
P.O. Box 2833
High Point, NC 27261

Robert Dalton Photography
1107 Countryside Drive
Highpoint, NC 27265

Models: **Najah Clinton, Forrest Daniel, Govan Faine, Lauren Faine, Marcelle Hunter, Kristi McGurk, Alex Maness**

THANK YOU ALL AND GOD BLESS YOU!!